Laura Walker

Your Real Estate Consultant For Life

Copyright © 2024 by Laura Walker

All rights reserved.

No portion of this book may be reproduced in any form without written permission from the publisher or author, except as permitted by U.S. copyright law.

Contents

Foreword — IV
by Joe Stumpf

Laura's Professional Accomplishments — VII

Overview — IX

1. Resilience Forged in Adversity — 1
   A Mother's Unintended Legacy

2. The Gift of Normalcy — 5
   A Father's Impact on Shaping Identity

3. The Synergy of Tax and Real Estate — 11
   Building Trust Through Preparation

4. The Ripple Effect of Integrity — 17
   A Legacy of Trust

5. Wisdom in Action — 22
   21 Lessons for Success in Real Estate, Finance, and Life

Foreword

by Joe Stumpf

It is a privilege to write the foreword for this remarkable book by Laura Walker, a woman who has dedicated 46 years to serving her clients in both real estate and tax preparation. Laura's dual expertise is a rarity in our industry, and her deep, enduring client relationships are a testament to her exceptional service.

Laura's story is not an easy one to tell. Her challenging relationship with her mother in early childhood could have defined her negatively, but instead, it became the crucible that forged her strength and empathy. I'm immensely proud of Laura's courage in sharing her story, recognizing how her experiences have shaped her into the professional she is today, and using them to help others.

In this book, Laura offers invaluable insights drawn from her life and career:

Chapter 1. Resilience Forged in Adversity: A Mother's Unintended Legacy

• How adversity can be transformed into professional strengths

• The power of resilience in overcoming life's challenges

• How childhood experiences can enhance empathy and problem-solving skills

Chapter 2. The Gift of Normalcy: A Father's Impact on Shaping Identity

• The importance of stability and its impact on personal development

• How a strong work ethic is cultivated and applied in professional life

• The value of seeing different perspectives in business and personal relationships

Chapter 3. The Synergy of Tax and Real Estate: Building Trust Through Preparation

• How diverse skills can create a unique and powerful professional offering

• The importance of thorough preparation in building client trust

• How to provide comprehensive financial guidance in real estate transactions

Chapter 4. The Ripple Effect of Integrity: A Legacy of Trust

• The long-term benefits of maintaining integrity in business

• How to build a reputation that attracts and retains clients

• The power of consistently doing the right thing, even when it's difficult

Chapter 5. Wisdom in Action: 21 Lessons for Success in Real Estate, Finance, and Life

• Practical strategies for success in real estate and financial planning

• How to apply life lessons to professional challenges

• Invaluable insights from 46 years of industry experience

I encourage you to dive deep into this book. Laura's wisdom, earned through years of experience and personal growth, is a treasure trove for anyone in real estate, finance, or simply navigating life's challenges. When it's time to buy or sell a home or when you need expert tax advice, I wholeheartedly recommend connecting with Laura. Her unique blend of expertise, empathy, and integrity is truly exceptional.

Joe Stumpf
Founder, By Referral Only

Laura's Professional Accomplisments

One Good Reason to Call Laura Walker: Experience IS Priceless

Calif Dept of Real Estate License # 00640079 46 years

Keller Williams Real Estate Services

Calif Dept of Real Estate Broker License since 2021

Member of National Association of Realtors® 46 years

Member of California Association of Realtors® 46 years

Income Tax Preparer Tested and Approved by IRS

IRS Enrolled Agent # 00100534-EA

Member of the National Association of Enrolled Agents

Member of California Society of Enrolled Agents

Professional Income Tax Preparer 28 years +

Tax Preparer for Tax Corp of America, Montrose 5 years

Another Good Reason to Call Laura Walker: The Bigger Picture

California Notary Public 24 years until 2019

Member of the National Notary Association 24 years until 2019

NNA Certified Loan-Signing Specialist 14 years until 2019

University of Southern California Accounting Degree 1995

Beta Gamma Sigma Honor Society since 1994

Golden Key National Honor Society since 1994

Passed CPA Exam 1996

Previous employment includes:

Du Pont Regional Sales Department, Burbank, Executive Assistant

RCA Sales Division, Hollywood, Executive Assistant

Beneficial Finance, Sunland, Glendale, and San Fernando, Cashier/Bookkeeper

Maybe the Best Reason to Call Laura Walker: Attitude

A job worth doing is worth doing right!

Professional Work Ethics, Customized Personal Service

You Can Put Laura's Education and Experience to Work for You!

818-248-4555

Laura@WalkerWorks123.com

Overview

Chapter 1. Resilience Forged in Adversity: A Mother's Unintended Legacy

You know, sometimes our greatest strengths come from the most unexpected places. In this chapter, I'll take you on a journey through my childhood – a time that wasn't always easy but shaped me in ways I'm only now beginning to fully appreciate. I'll share how growing up with a young, single mother taught me resilience, problem-solving, and self-reliance. These aren't just stories from my past; they're the foundation of how I approach my work in real estate and tax preparation today. You'll see how the challenges I faced as a child have given me a unique ability to empathize with my clients and navigate complex situations. Whether you're facing your own challenges or just curious about how early experiences shape us, this chapter will give you insights into turning adversity into strength. By the end, you'll understand how these early lessons have allowed me to offer a level of service and understanding that goes beyond typical real estate and tax preparation. Trust me, this journey of resilience is one you won't want to miss.

Chapter 2. The Gift of Normalcy: A Father's Impact on Shaping Identity

Ever wonder how a brief period in your life can shape your entire future? That's what this chapter is all about. I'll take you through the years I spent with my father – times that gave me a glimpse of normalcy and stability I'd never known before. You'll see how his work ethic, sense of justice, and the simple act of providing a stable home left an indelible mark on me. This isn't just a story about my past; it's a blueprint for how I approach my work today. You'll learn how these experiences taught me the value of hard work, the importance of standing up for what's right, and the power of creating a secure environment – all lessons I now use to benefit my clients. Whether you're dealing with your own family dynamics or looking to understand how childhood experiences shape professional approaches, this chapter offers valuable insights. By the end, you'll see how these formative experiences have influenced my unique approach to real estate and tax preparation. Trust me, this exploration of a father's impact is a journey you won't want to miss.

Chapter 3. The Synergy of Tax and Real Estate: Building Trust Through Preparation

Have you ever wondered how seemingly unrelated skills can come together to create something truly unique? That's exactly what this chapter is about. I'll take you on my journey of discovering how my background in tax preparation perfectly complemented my real estate career. You'll see how this unexpected combination allows me to offer my clients a level of service that goes far beyond what most real estate agents can provide. I'll share stories of how this dual expertise has helped clients make smarter decisions, save money, and secure their financial futures. You'll learn about my approach to preparation and how it builds unshakeable trust with clients. Whether you're considering a career change, looking for a unique edge in your field, or simply curious about how diverse skills can come together, this chapter offers valuable insights. By the end, you'll understand why my clients see me not just as a real estate agent or tax preparer but as a trusted consultant. Trust me, this exploration of synergy and preparation is a journey you won't want to miss.

Chapter 4. The Ripple Effect of Integrity: A Legacy of Trust

Ever wondered how a single principle can shape an entire career and touch countless lives? That's what this chapter is all about. I'll take you through my journey of building a career on the foundation of integrity. You'll see how this commitment has not only shaped my business practices but has created a ripple effect that extends far beyond my immediate clients. I'll share stories of times when integrity cost me in the short term but paid dividends in the long run. You'll learn about the challenges of maintaining high ethical standards in a competitive industry and the unexpected rewards it brings. Whether you're starting your career, facing ethical dilemmas, or simply curious about the power of principles in business, this chapter offers valuable insights. By the end, you'll understand why I believe integrity isn't just a personal virtue but a powerful business model. Trust me, this exploration of the far-reaching impacts of integrity is a journey you won't want to miss.

Chapter 5. Wisdom in Action: 21 Lessons for Success in Real Estate, Finance, and Life

Ready for a treasure trove of wisdom that can transform your approach to real estate, income tax, and life itself? That's exactly what this chapter offers. I'll share with you 21 key lessons I've learned over my 46-year career – lessons that have not only shaped my success but have also helped countless clients achieve their dreams. From embracing resilience and cultivating self-reliance to the power of empathy and the importance of continuous learning, each lesson is packed with practical insights you can apply immediately. Whether you're buying your first home, planning for retirement, or simply looking to improve your income tax savvy, you'll find valuable advice here. I'll share real-life examples of how these lessons have played out in my career and in my clients' lives. By the end of this chapter, you'll have a toolkit of strategies to navigate the complex worlds of real estate and income taxes with confidence. Trust me, these 21 lessons are the distilled wisdom of a lifetime – you won't want to miss them.

Chapter One

Resilience Forged in Adversity

A Mother's Unintended Legacy

As I sit here, reflecting on my journey in real estate and tax preparation, I can't help but trace the roots of my success back to my childhood. It's a story I don't often share, but one that has shaped me in ways I'm only now beginning to fully appreciate. You see, my early years weren't typical - they were a crash course in resilience, self-reliance, and problem-solving. While I wouldn't wish my experiences on anyone, I've come to realize that they've given me unique tools that I now use every day to help my clients navigate their own complex journeys in real estate and income tax.

The Early Years: Unexpected Independence

I was just six years old when my parent's marriage fell apart. My mother was young - only 20 when I was born - and suddenly found herself a single parent to three small children in an era when that was far from socially acceptable. I have two younger siblings - a sister who was three and a brother who was two at the time. Almost overnight, our world changed dramatically.

By the time I was seven and a half, I had become what I can only describe now as a "little adult." My mother, struggling to provide for us, was often absent - working long hours, day and night. We were left to our own devices, with no real guidance on what to do or where to go. It might sound alarming to modern ears, but back then, it wasn't uncommon to see a seven-year-old, a four-year-old, and a three-year-old walking around town unsupervised, stopping by the library and seeking out our own adventures. In fact, we were out seeking adventures daily.

The Invisible Skills of Survival

Looking back, I realize now that this period of my life was laying the groundwork for skills I use every day in my professional life. Problem-solving became second nature. If my siblings were hungry and the cupboards were bare, it was up to me to figure out a solution. (As a young adult, I realized my brain doesn't recognize hunger like other people. Eventually, thinking back, I figured out why.) When shoes didn't fit right, I learned to improvise - taking out the laces and tying them up in new ways to make them work and cutting the toe part open a bit. Eventually, we gave up on shoes.

These may seem like small things, but they taught me invaluable lessons about resourcefulness and creative thinking. Today, when I'm helping a client navigate a complex real estate transaction or find innovative ways to maximize their tax benefits, I'm drawing on those same skills I developed as a child.

The Warmth of Ingenuity

One memory that stands out vividly is how we dealt with cold nights in Michigan. We didn't always have proper heating, so we had to get creative. We'd put on all the warm clothes we had, build a tent out of blankets, and huddle together inside. At the time, I didn't know anything about body heat - I was just operating on instinct, trying to keep my younger siblings warm and safe.

Now, when I think about that experience, I see a powerful metaphor for what I do in my career. Just as I created a warm, safe space for my siblings, I strive to create a sense of security, comfort, and calm for my clients as they navigate the often stressful process of buying or selling a home or dealing with complex tax issues.

The Unexpected Gift of Adversity

It wasn't until I became a parent myself that I truly began to understand the challenges my mother faced. As a single mother in an era when that was frowned upon, she was doing her best to provide for us in incredibly difficult circumstances. While her approach to parenting was inconsistent and often left us to fend for ourselves, I can now appreciate the work ethic and determination she modeled.

Mom worked hard, sacrificing her time with us to ensure we had a roof over our heads so we had a place to call home. This "purposeful sacrifice," as I've come to think of it, taught me the value of hard work and perseverance - qualities that have served me well in my career.

Empathy Born from Experience

My childhood experiences have given me a unique ability to empathize with my clients, especially those going through challenging times. When a client is stressed about the tax impact of a major financial decision or feeling overwhelmed by the complexities of a real estate transaction, I can truly relate. I know what it's like to face uncertainty and to have to make difficult decisions with limited information.

This empathy allows me to connect with my clients on a deeper level. I'm not just their real estate agent or tax preparer - I become a trusted advisor, someone who understands their struggles and is committed to helping them navigate through them, looking ahead before taking one step at a time with eyes wide open. I sincerely believe it's my job to provide accurate and thorough information so my clients can make the best decisions for their own lives.

The Foundation of Client Service

In my work, I'm known for my meticulous preparation and attention to detail. Clients often comment on how calm and reassuring I am, even in high-stress situations. What they might not realize is that this approach is directly tied to my childhood experiences.

When you've had to be responsible for yourself and others from a young age, you learn the importance of thinking ahead, anticipating problems, and being prepared for anything. This has translated into my professional life as a commitment to thorough research, careful planning, and always being ready with solutions before problems arise. I call that problem-prevention, which is usually behind the scenes.

A Legacy of Strength

While my childhood was far from ideal, I've come to see it as a source of strength rather than a limitation. Few young children have the total freedom I had to step outside, walk for miles in all directions, and discover the world around me every day; it was fun. The resilience, problem-solving skills, and empathy I developed have become the cornerstones of my approach to serving my clients.

When I work with a buyer or seller, they're not just getting my professional expertise - they're benefiting from a lifetime of experiences in overcoming adversity, finding creative solutions, and persevering through challenges. It's this unique background that allows me to offer a level of service and understanding that goes beyond typical real estate and tax preparation.

As I continue in my career, I carry with me the lessons learned from those early years. They remind me daily of the importance of compassion, the power of perseverance, and the incredible resilience of the human spirit. These are the gifts from my past that I silently share with every client I serve, helping them navigate their own journeys with confidence and care.

Chapter Two

The Gift of Normalcy

A Father's Impact on Shaping Identity

As I reflect on my journey in real estate and tax preparation, I can't help but think about the profound impact my father had on shaping who I am today. While my early childhood was marked by uncertainty and responsibility beyond my years, my father's influence provided a stark contrast that ultimately helped me develop a more balanced approach to life and business.

A Young Father's Journey

My father was just 25 when I was born, fresh from serving in World War II. It's funny. For years, I thought he had served in Korea, but when I asked him about it as an adult, he corrected me - it was Austria. He never wanted to talk much about his time in the war, but I remember a photograph he kept in his workshop of him with two buddies. I always had a feeling those were friends he'd lost, though I never asked. Some things, I learned, are better left unspoken.

At 25, he was far from ready for the responsibilities of marriage and fatherhood. As he often said, "You do what you got to do." This simple phrase would become a guiding principle in my life, shaping my work ethic and approach to challenges.

The Fight for Custody

When my parents' marriage fell apart, my father did something that surprised me - he fought like crazy for custody of us kids. It wasn't the norm back then for fathers to seek custody, but he was determined. I remember those times vividly because they were when my mother would actually hire a babysitter to stay with us (which substantially curbed our freedom). It was as if Mom suddenly realized she needed to step up her game.

A Taste of Childhood

Just before I turned eight, my father won custody of us for a brief period - about a school year. This time with him was transformative. For the first time, I didn't have to be responsible for my younger siblings. There was always someone there to take care of us.

I got to experience what it was like to just be a little girl. My dad bought me a record player, and I could listen to music and play with Barbie dolls. I discovered I liked puzzles and drawing pictures. It was a stark contrast to the responsibilities I'd shouldered before, and it gave me a glimpse of what childhood could be.

When the Friend of the Court, a name which baffled me, decided we should live with Mom again, Dad continued his fight for custody even more. Perhaps that was why Mom moved us to California, which covered 6th and 7th grades for me. Just before 8th grade, I decided it was time for me to step up. I was determined to live with Dad in Michigan, even if I had to walk. I knew if I started the journey, Dad would come to get me. It didn't come to that. I lived with Dad from 8th – 11th grade. Because I missed my sister and brother, I decided to spend my last year as a minor, 12th grade, in California to be sure they were okay. Two weeks after high school graduation, as an honor student, I was truly independent, on my own, and determined to be a self-reliant adult.

The Value of Hard Work and Stability

My time living with my father left a lasting impression. He worked incredibly hard, leaving for work at 3:30 every morning (not a typo) and returning home around 5:30 in the evening. He even worked half-days on Saturdays.

This experience taught me the value of stability and the importance of creating a secure environment. In my real estate career, I've carried this lesson with me, always striving to help my clients find not just houses but homes where they can create their own sense of security and normalcy.

The Impact on My Professional Life

My father's influence has shaped my approach to work in numerous ways. Like him, I believe in doing what needs to be done, no matter how challenging. During tax season, when I'm juggling both real estate and tax preparation, I often think of my father's work ethic. The long hours and dedication he showed have become a part of my own professional DNA. But I've also learned the importance of balance, something I strive to help my clients understand as they navigate the complex worlds of real estate and taxes.

Embracing Change and Adaptability

Growing up with a young father taught me the value of adaptability. He was learning and growing alongside us, facing challenges head-on. This experience has made me more open to change and new ideas in my career.

In a field that's constantly evolving, this adaptability has been invaluable. It allows me to provide my clients with the most up-to-date advice and strategies, whether we're discussing the latest market trends or navigating recent changes in tax law.

Building Relationships and Trust

Perhaps one of the most significant lessons I learned from my father was the importance of fighting for what's right. His determination to be part of our lives, even when societal norms were against him, showed me the value of perseverance and standing up for what I believe in.

In my real estate and tax preparation businesses, this translates to always advocating for my client's best interests. I'm not afraid to go the extra mile, to dig deeper into the complex tax implications of a real estate transaction, or to negotiate tirelessly on behalf of a buyer or seller.

A Sense of Justice and Doing Right

My father had a strong sense of justice, a trait that has deeply influenced my business ethics. Dad had a sense of justice as well. Here's a young man who is enthusiastic and has a lot of energy, and there's this part of him that said, 'You know what? I put things right with my kids. I have to fight for custody of my kids.'

This sense of right and wrong has become a cornerstone of my business philosophy. I believe in always doing the right thing, even when it's challenging or when no one is watching. This integrity has helped me build trust with my clients and establish a reputation for honesty and fairness in both my real estate and tax preparation businesses.

The Gift of a Different Perspective

One of the most valuable things my father gave me was a different perspective on life. From age 6 to almost 8, I only knew one way of being - the independent, responsible caretaker. But when my father gained custody, I got my first glimpse that things could be different.

This ability to see different perspectives has been crucial in my career. It allows me to help my clients see possibilities they might not have considered, whether it's a creative solution to a tax issue or an innovative approach to marketing their property.

Connecting with Clients

The experience of having a young, relatable father has enhanced my ability to connect with a wide range of clients. Just as there was less of a hierarchical relationship between my father and me, I strive to create a collaborative, approachable relationship with my clients.

Whether I'm working with first-time homebuyers, seasoned investors, or clients navigating complex tax situations, I can adapt my communication style to meet their needs. This skill, honed through my unique childhood experiences, helps me build strong, lasting relationships with my clients.

Balancing Work and Life

Watching my father juggle his career and his responsibilities taught me valuable lessons about work-life balance. In my own career, I've learned to prioritize effectively, managing the demands of both my real estate and tax preparation businesses while still making time for my personal life. Yes, the balance often is skewed because my work life and my personal life have always been intertwined. But I'm still aware of balance and its impact.

This understanding of balance also informs how I advise my clients. I help them consider not just the financial implications of their real estate decisions but also how these choices will impact their overall quality of life.

The Lasting Impact of a Father's Love

My father's influence on my life and career cannot be overstated. His work ethic, sense of justice, and the normalcy he provided have all shaped the professional I am today. From him, I learned the importance of hard work, the value of fighting for what's right, and the power of providing stability and security.

These lessons have become the foundation of my approach to both real estate and tax preparation. They've helped me build a career based on integrity, hard work, and a deep commitment to my client's well-being.

As I continue in my career, I carry with me the lessons learned from those early years with my father. They remind me daily of the importance of perseverance, the power of a different perspective, and the incredible impact we can have when we fight for what's right. These are the gifts from my father that I now share with every client I serve, helping them navigate their own journeys with confidence, integrity, and a sense of possibility.

Chapter Three

The Synergy of Tax and Real Estate

Building Trust Through Preparation

A Serendipitous Start

You know, it's funny how life has a way of leading you down paths you never expected. If you had told me years ago that I'd end up with a career that perfectly blended real estate and tax preparation, I would have laughed. But here I am, and I wouldn't have it any other way. Let me tell you how it all came together.

It all started with my tax business. I remember sitting at my dining table, watching my tax preparer work his magic with numbers. For two years in a row, he looked up from his papers and said, "You should become a tax preparer. You're so organized. You're so thorough. You could do this." At first, I brushed it off, but the seed was planted.

The Power of Recognition and the Leap into Real Estate

Have you ever had someone see potential in you that you didn't see in yourself? It's a powerful thing. Those words from my tax preparer stuck with me, and eventually, I thought, "Why not?" I decided to give it a try, and I started my tax business without giving up my regular paycheck job. It was the perfect way to dip my toes into entrepreneurship without diving headfirst into uncertain waters.

A couple of years into my tax business, fate took another interesting turn. I found myself on a first date with a real estate office manager. When he arrived, I asked if he would mind sitting in the living room. I had three more quick calls to make to potential new tax clients. He could hear my proactive approach to follow-up. "You should get your real estate license," he suggested over dinner. I was taken aback. "No, I can't," I protested. "I'm not sales. I promise I'm not sales. I don't know a thing about it." But he saw something in me that I didn't see in myself. "You're already doing it," he insisted.

Six months later, I took the leap and enrolled in real estate school, quitting my steady job. It was a terrifying yet exhilarating decision, one that required a mix of fear, excitement, and a lot of faith. But deep down, I knew it was the right move.

Merging Two Worlds: The Perfect Blend

Initially, I saw my tax business and my new career in real estate as two separate entities. Tax preparation brought in extra money during tax season, while real estate was my new full-time focus. But over time, something beautiful happened—the two worlds began to merge. It wasn't a conscious decision; it just... happened. And looking back, I can see how perfectly these two fields complement each other. It's like they were always meant to be together, at least in my career.

The Synergy of Tax and Real Estate

Now, let me tell you why this combination is so powerful. When you're buying or selling a home, it's not just about the property itself. It's about how that transaction fits into your overall financial picture. And that's where my tax knowledge comes in handy.

For buyers, I'm not just helping them find a home within their budget. I'm helping them understand how this purchase will affect their overall financial situation. We're talking about tax liabilities, potential deductions, the whole nine yards. It's like putting together a financial puzzle, and I get to help my clients see the whole picture.

For sellers, we look at strategies to minimize tax burdens, navigate capital gains exceptions, and find the best ways to reinvest profits. It's not just about getting the best price for their home; it's about making sure that money works as hard as possible for them once it's in their pocket.

The Long-Term Impact of Dual Expertise

What excites me most about this dual expertise is the long-term impact I can have on my clients' lives. A real estate transaction isn't just a one-time deal. It has ripple effects that can last for years, even decades. When I sit down with a client, we're not just talking about mortgage interest deductions or property tax deductions for the current year. We're looking at the benefits of holding the property under certain types of ownership and different structures that could benefit them down the line. It's like planting financial seeds together, and I get to help my clients watch them grow over time.

Preparation as a Foundation for Trust

Through all these experiences, one thing has stood out: the importance of preparation. You know, throughout my career in real estate and tax preparation, I've come to realize that there's one skill that sets me apart more than any other: preparation. It's not just about being ready for client meetings or having the right paperwork in order. It's about a mindset, a way of approaching every aspect of my work that allows me to provide the best possible service to my clients.

Many don't see the hours of work that go on behind the scenes. It's not just about phone calls and meetings—there's so much more to it, and that's where the real work happens. I have what I call my "Next" list. It used to be a to-do list, which I'm thankful never got done. I've found that framing it as "Next" keeps me focused on fluid priorities, moving forward, and as prepared as possible for what's coming.

Building Trust Through Knowledge and Transparency

If there's one thing that defines my approach to both real estate and tax preparation, it's education. I believe wholeheartedly in empowering my clients through knowledge. It's not about making decisions for them—it's about giving them the information they need to make the best choices for themselves and their families.

Transparency is key in this process. When you're open and honest about every aspect of a transaction—from market conditions to potential challenges—you create a foundation of trust that's unshakeable. I remember working with a couple who were first-time homebuyers. They were nervous and overwhelmed by the process. But as we went through each step, explaining everything in detail, I could see them relax. By the time we closed on their home, they weren't just clients—they were friends who trusted me implicitly.

The Consultant, Not the Salesperson

From the beginning, I was adamant that I wasn't a salesperson. And you know what? I still stand by that. I'm not here to sell houses or tax services. I'm here to consult, to educate, to guide. I'll never forget a conversation I had with a client after closing a particularly complex deal. They looked at me and said, "Laura, you're not just our real estate agent. You're our financial guide." Although I don't have financial advisor credentials or that license, I knew what my clients meant. That moment crystallized exactly what I strive to be for my clients. And sometimes, I do guide my clients toward specialized financial advisors and/or attorneys.

Mastery of Numbers: The Backbone of Preparation

A crucial part of my preparation is my mastery of numbers. In both real estate and tax preparation, understanding and tracking all the critical numbers is essential. It's not just about being good with math—it's about understanding what those numbers mean for my clients' lives and futures. This mastery allows me to offer insights that many other real estate agents can't. I can help my clients understand not just the purchase price of a home but how it fits into their overall financial picture. I can explain tax implications, potential deductions, and long-term financial impacts. This comprehensive understanding builds a deep level of trust with my clients.

Changing Lives Through Preparation

It's a powerful thing when a client tells you that you've changed their life. I've been fortunate enough to hear that more than once, and each time, it reminds me of why I do what I do. By being thoroughly prepared, I'm able to guide my clients through some of the most significant financial decisions of their lives. Whether it's helping a first-time homebuyer understand the intricacies of a mortgage or assisting a retiree in minimizing their tax burden when selling their long-time home, my preparation allows me to offer solutions that can truly be life-changing.

The Never-Ending Learning Journey

Here's a little secret: I love being in teaching mode because it keeps me learning, too. The real estate market is always changing. Tax laws are constantly being updated. To stay on top of my game, I have to be a perpetual student. I'm constantly taking courses, attending seminars and webinars, and staying up-to-date with the latest trends and regulations. It's exhausting sometimes, I won't lie. But it's also exhilarating. There's always something new to learn, always a way to better serve my clients.

A Legacy of Trust and Service

Looking back over the years, I'm amazed at how many lives I've touched through this unique combination of real estate and tax preparation. Between both of my businesses, I've helped somewhere between 75 to 100 people a year, sometimes even up to 150. Over the course of 46 years, that's a lot of people!

But you know what's even more rewarding than the numbers? It's the relationships I've built. Many of my clients have been with me for years, trusting me with both their real estate needs and their taxes. It's like I've become a part of their financial family. As I look to the future, I'm filled with a sense of purpose and excitement.

The worlds of real estate and income taxes are always evolving, and I'm committed to evolving with them. But no matter what changes come our way, one thing will remain constant: my dedication to serving my clients with integrity, empathy, and expertise.

A Call to Action

To anyone considering a career in real estate or income tax preparation—or both!—I say this: embrace the opportunity to make a real difference in people's lives. It's not just about houses or numbers. It's about helping people build their dreams, secure their futures, and navigate the complex worlds of real estate and taxes with confidence.

Remember, success isn't just about what you achieve for yourself. It's about the lives you touch, the trust you build, and the positive change you create in the world. That's the true measure of a fulfilling career, and it's what gets me excited to start each new day.

So, are you ready to take on the challenge? Are you ready to become not just a professional but a trusted advisor, a teacher, or a guide? The journey isn't always easy, but I promise you, it's worth every step. Let's make a difference: one client, one home, one tax return at a time.

Chapter Four

The Ripple Effect of Integrity

A Legacy of Trust

As I reflect on my career in real estate and tax preparation, I'm struck by how a simple principle has shaped not just my professional life but my entire approach to serving others. It's a principle that goes beyond business strategies or market knowledge. It's about something far more fundamental: integrity.

The Power of Consistency

You know, in these industries, it's easy to get caught up in the latest trends or marketing gimmicks. But I've found that what truly sets me apart is consistency in doing the right thing, even when no one is watching. It's not about grand gestures or one-time acts of kindness. It's about the small, everyday decisions that add up over time.

I remember a client once telling me, "Laura, what amazes me is how you're the same person whether we're in a high-stakes negotiation or just catching up over coffee." That comment stuck with me because it encapsulated exactly what I strive for – a consistency of character that builds trust over time.

The Unseen Impact

What fascinates me most about integrity is its ripple effect. When you consistently do the right thing, it doesn't just impact your immediate interactions. It spreads outward, touching lives in ways you might never even realize.

I recall a situation where I advised a client against purchasing a property that would have brought me a substantial commission. It wasn't an easy decision, but I knew the property had issues that would cause problems down the line. Years later, that same client referred their daughter to me, saying, "I trust Laura with my child's future because she once prioritized my wellbeing over her own profit."

That's the power of integrity. It's not just about one transaction or one client relationship. It's about building a legacy of trust that extends far beyond your immediate sphere of influence.

The Courage to Stand Alone

Maintaining integrity isn't always easy, especially when cutting corners can sometimes lead to quick profits. There have been times when I've had to stand alone, refusing to participate in practices that I felt were ethically questionable.

Sometimes, I see or hear about what I consider to be misleading marketing tactics. I typically check with colleagues who I respect. Is this a common thing now? Is it even ethical? Then I think it through myself. Does it pass the test: is it the right thing to do? If not, it won't last long, and I know I can't look my clients in the eye if I compromise my principles. I love it when someone tours a property I have listed for sale and then says to me, "Your description of this property on the internet is perfect; the words you wrote are exactly what I saw and felt as I walked through."

Doing the right thing all of the time can be a lonely stance, and I won't pretend it never costs me some business. But over time, something remarkable happened. Clients started seeking me out specifically because they had heard about my ethics. They wanted someone they could trust implicitly with one of the biggest financial decisions of their lives or their annual tax report of some very personal details.

Integrity as a Business Model

What I've learned over the years is that integrity isn't just a personal virtue – it's a viable and powerful business model. In a world where trust is increasingly scarce, being known as someone who consistently does the right thing becomes your most valuable asset.

This approach has shaped every aspect of my business. From the way I structure my fees to ensure transparency to the honest advice I give, even when it might not lead to an immediate sale – every decision is filtered through the lens of integrity.

And you know what? It's not just good ethics – it's good business. The long-term relationships I've built, the referrals I've received, and the reputation I've established are all direct results of this unwavering commitment to doing right by my clients.

Teaching Integrity

One of the most rewarding aspects of my career has been the opportunity to mentor younger real estate agents and instill in them this same principle. I often tell them, "Your integrity is your real estate. Guard it, cultivate it, and it will yield returns far greater than any commission."

I've seen young agents struggle with the pressure to compromise and take shortcuts for quick gains. My advice to them is always the same: play the long game. Build your career on a foundation of trust and integrity, and you'll never have to worry about job security or where your next client is coming from.

The Personal Cost and Reward

Living with integrity isn't always easy. There have been times when it's cost me – financially, professionally, even personally. But the peace of mind it brings, the ability to sleep soundly at night knowing you've done right by your clients and yourself – that's priceless.

Moreover, the personal growth that comes from consistently choosing the right path, even when it's difficult, has been immeasurable. It's shaped me not just as a professional, but as a person. The resilience, the clarity of purpose, the inner strength – these are the true rewards of a life lived with integrity.

A Call to Higher Standards

As I look to the future of the real estate and income tax prep industries, my hope is that we can collectively raise the bar when it comes to ethical stan- dards. Imagine real estate and income tax services sectors where integrity isn't the exception but the norm, where clients don't have to wonder if they're getting honest advice or if their interests are truly being put first.

It's not just a pipedream. It starts with each of us making a commitment to integrity, not just in the big moments but in the small, everyday decisions. It's about creating a culture where doing the right thing is celebrated and expected.

To my colleagues in these industries, I say this: let's be the change we want to see. Let's build businesses and careers that we can be proud of, not just for the financial success they bring but for the positive impact they have on the lives of our clients and communities.

The Ultimate Legacy

As I reflect on my career, I realize that the houses I've sold and the tax returns I've prepared – are not my true legacy. My legacy is the trust I've built, the lives I've positively impacted, and the example I've set for ethical business practices.

To anyone reading this, whether you're in real estate, finance, or any other field, I urge you to consider the power of integrity in your own life and career. It's not always the easiest path, but I can tell you from experience, it's the most rewarding.

Remember, at the end of the day, your reputation – built on a foundation of integrity – is your most valuable asset. Guard it fiercely, nurture it consistently, and watch as it opens doors and creates opportunities you never thought possible.

In a world that often seems to prioritize short-term gains over long-term values, let's be the ones who stand firm in our principles. Let's be the ones who prove that integrity isn't just the right way to live – it's the smartest way to succeed.

Chapter Five

Wisdom in Action

21 Lessons for Success in Real Estate, Finance, and Life

1. Embrace Resilience in the Face of Adversity

You know, life hasn't always been easy for me, but I've learned that resilience is a superpower we all have within us. When you're facing challenges in your home-buying journey or struggling with a complex tax situation, remember that every obstacle is an opportunity to grow stronger. I've seen clients transform their lives by embracing resilience. Whether it's bouncing back from a failed offer on a dream home or navigating an IRS audit, your ability to stay positive and keep moving forward will serve you well. Don't be afraid of setbacks; use them as stepping stones. The resilience you develop will not only help you achieve your immediate goals but will also serve you in all aspects of your life.

2. Cultivate Self-Reliance for Empowered Decision-Making

I learned early on that self-reliance is key to success, and it's a lesson I share with all my clients. When you're buying or selling a home or managing your taxes, it's easy to feel overwhelmed and want to rely entirely on experts. But here's the thing: while professional guidance is valuable, your own understanding and involvement are crucial. Take the time to educate yourself about the process. Ask questions, do your research, and trust your instincts. The more self-reliant you become, the more confident you'll be in your decisions. I've seen clients transform from being hesitant and unsure to becoming savvy homeowners and financially astute individuals. Remember, you're the expert on your own needs and goals. Embrace that knowledge and use it to guide your choices.

3. Sharpen Your Problem-Solving Skills

Life is full of unexpected challenges, especially in real estate and taxes. The ability to solve problems creatively and efficiently is invaluable. I encourage you to approach each obstacle as a puzzle to be solved rather than a roadblock. When you're house hunting, don't just see a property for what it is but for what it could be with a little problem-solving ingenuity. In your financial planning, look for creative solutions to maximize your tax benefits. I've watched clients turn potential deal-breakers into opportunities simply by shifting their perspectives and flexing their problem-solving muscles. Cultivate this skill in your daily life, and you'll find yourself better equipped to handle whatever comes your way in your home buying, selling, or tax preparation journey.

4. The Value of Preparation

Let me tell you, preparation is everything, and it's a lesson that can change your life. Whether you're buying a home, selling a property, or getting ready for tax season, being prepared puts you miles ahead. I've heard, "The way you spell love is P-R-E-P-A-R-E." When you're house hunting, do your research on neighborhoods, school districts, and market trends before you even start looking at properties. If you're selling, prepare your home meticulously for showings. For taxes, keep your records organized year-round. I've seen clients save thousands of dollars and avoid countless headaches simply by being well-prepared. Remember, success loves preparation. The time you invest in getting ready will pay off tenfold in smoother transactions and better outcomes.

5. Embrace Continuous Learning

In my years of experience, I've learned that the moment you think you know it all is the moment you start falling behind. The real estate market and tax laws are constantly changing, and to serve you best, I need to stay on top of these changes. The same principle applies to you. Whether you're a first-time homebuyer or a seasoned investor, there's always something new to learn. Stay curious, ask questions, and seek out information. Attend workshops, read industry publications, and don't be afraid to learn from your mistakes. I've seen clients transform their financial futures simply by committing to ongoing education. Remember, knowledge is power, especially when it comes to making significant financial decisions.

6. The Power of Empathy

Empathy isn't just a nice-to-have in this business; it's essential. I learned early on that understanding and relating to my clients' situations, fears, and dreams is crucial to serving them well. When you're dealing with a real estate agent or tax preparer, look for someone who truly listens and puts themselves in your shoes. As a client, practice empathy too. Understanding the challenges of the other party in a real estate transaction can lead to smoother negotiations and better outcomes. I've seen deals saved and relationships strengthened through the simple act of empathy. Remember, buying a home or managing your taxes isn't just a financial transaction – it's a deeply personal experience. Approaching it with empathy can make all the difference.

7. The Importance of Integrity

Let me tell you, integrity is the cornerstone of everything I do, and it should be for you, too. In real estate and tax preparation, you're dealing with people's homes and financial futures. There's no room for cutting corners or bending the truth. Always do the right thing, even when no one is watching. I've seen clients achieve incredible success simply by sticking to their principles and being honest in all their dealings. When you're buying or selling a home, be transparent about your situation and expectations.

When preparing your taxes, report everything accurately. It might seem tempting to take shortcuts, but in the long run, integrity pays off. It builds trust, enhances your reputation, and leads to lasting relationships. Remember, your integrity is your most valuable asset.

8. The Value of Clear Communication

I can't stress enough how important clear communication is in business. Whether you're negotiating a home purchase, explaining your financial situation to a tax preparer, or discussing terms with a client, being able to articulate your thoughts clearly and listen actively is crucial. I've seen deals fall apart due to misunderstandings and succeed because of clear, open dialogue. When you're working with professionals or clients, don't be afraid to ask for clarification if something isn't clear. Be specific about your needs and expectations. And remember, communication is a two-way street. Listen as much as you speak. The better you communicate, the smoother everything will be, and the more satisfying your results will be.

9. The Power of Adaptability

If there's one thing I've learned in my years of business, it's that change is constant. The real estate market fluctuates, tax laws evolve, and client needs shift. To succeed, you need to be adaptable. I've seen clients thrive by being flexible in their home search, open to new tax strategies, and willing to adjust their plans when circumstances change. When you're buying or selling a home, be prepared to pivot if market conditions shift. In tax planning, be ready to adapt your strategies as laws change. Rigidity can cost you opportunities, while adaptability can open doors you never knew existed. Embrace change and stay flexible, and you'll be better equipped to navigate the complex worlds of real estate and income tax.

10. The Strength in Building Relationships

You know, relationships are everything. It's not just about closing a deal or filing a tax return; it's about building lasting connections. I've seen time and time again how strong relationships lead to repeat business, referrals, and opportunities I never saw coming. When you're working with a real estate agent or tax preparer, look for someone who values relationship-building. And as a client, invest in those relationships, too. Be honest, be reliable, and show appreciation. I've had clients who've been with me for decades, and it's because we've built a foundation of trust and mutual respect. Remember, in real estate and tax preparation, your network is your net worth. Nurture your relationships, and they'll nurture your success.

11. The Importance of Financial Literacy

Let me tell you that understanding the financial aspects of real estate and taxes is crucial. I've seen too many people make costly mistakes simply because they didn't understand the financial implications of their decisions. Whether you're buying a home, selling a property, or planning your taxes, take the time to educate yourself about the financial aspects involved. Learn about mortgage terms, tax deductions, capital gains, and investment strategies. The more financially literate you are, the better decisions you'll make. I've watched clients transform their financial futures by committing to improving their financial knowledge. Remember, knowledge is power, especially when it comes to your money.

12. The Value of Patience

In this fast-paced world, patience is a virtue that's often overlooked, but it's so important in business. I've seen clients miss out on great opportunities because they rushed into decisions, and I've seen others reap huge rewards because they were patient enough to wait for the right moment. When you're house hunting, don't settle for a property that doesn't meet your needs just because you're in a hurry. When you're selling, don't jump at the first offer if it doesn't align with your goals. In tax planning, sometimes waiting for the right time to make a financial move can save you thousands. Remember, good things come to those who wait. Be patient, stay focused on your long-term goals, and trust the process.

13. The Power of Attention to Detail

You know, in real estate and tax preparation, the devil really is in the details. I can't tell you how many times I've seen small oversights lead to big problems. Whether you're reviewing a purchase agreement, preparing your tax returns, or evaluating a property, pay close attention to every detail. Double-check everything. I always encourage my clients to read every document thoroughly, even if it seems tedious. Don't be afraid to ask questions about things you don't understand. I've had clients save thousands of dollars or avoid potential legal issues simply by being meticulous. Remember, when it comes to your home and your finances, there's no such thing as being too careful.

14. The Importance of Timing

Timing can make all the difference in real estate and tax planning. I've seen clients achieve amazing results by making moves at just the right moment, and I've seen others miss out because their timing was off. In real estate, understanding market cycles can help you buy or sell at the most advantageous time. In tax planning, knowing when to realize gains or losses or when to make certain financial moves can significantly impact your tax liability. Always be aware of timing in your decision-making process. Stay informed about market trends and tax deadlines. Remember, it's not just about making the right move; it's about making the right move at the right time.

15. The Value of Long-Term Thinking

In my years of experience, I've learned that the most successful clients are those who think long-term. It's easy to get caught up in short-term gains or immediate gratification, but real wealth and stability come from thinking ahead. When you're buying a home, consider not just your current needs but where you might be in 5 or 10 years. In tax planning, look beyond just this year's return and consider strategies that will benefit you in the long run. I've seen clients make decisions they later regretted because they didn't consider the long-term implications. Always ask yourself, "How will this decision affect me in the future?" Remember, your home and your finances are long-term investments. Treat them as such, and you'll see much better results over time.

16. The Power of Networking

Let me tell you that your network can be your greatest asset in real estate and financial planning. I've seen clients find their dream homes, secure great deals, and uncover fantastic investment opportunities simply because they were well-connected. Build relationships not just with real estate professionals and financial advisors but also with other homeowners, investors, and business owners. Attend local real estate meetups, join finance-focused groups, and don't be shy about talking to people about your goals. You never know who might have the information or connection you need. I always encourage my clients to expand their networks, and I've watched it pay off time and time again. Remember, in this business, it's often not just what you know but who you know.

17. The Importance of Work-Life Balance

I learned this lesson the hard way, and it's one I always share with my clients. It's easy to get caught up in the hustle, especially when you're in the midst of a big real estate transaction or preparing for tax season. But burning out won't serve you or your goals. I've seen clients make poor decisions because they were exhausted or stressed. Take time to recharge, spend time with loved ones, and pursue interests outside of your financial goals. A balanced life leads to clearer thinking and better decision-making. When you're house hunting or working on your taxes, set boundaries and take breaks. Remember, your home and your finances are meant to enhance your life, not consume it.

18. The Value of Diversification

Don't put all your eggs in one basket - that's a lesson I've seen play out countless times in both real estate and tax planning. Diversification is key to managing risk and maximizing opportunities. In real estate, this might mean investing in different types of properties or in various locations. In financial planning, it could involve a mix of investment strategies or tax-saving approaches. I've had clients weather economic downturns much better than others because they had diversified portfolios. Always look for ways to spread your risk and explore different opportunities. Remember, diversification isn't just about protecting yourself from loss; it's about positioning yourself for multiple avenues of growth.

19. The Power of Authenticity

You know, in this business, being genuine goes a long way. I've learned that trying to be someone you're not or pretending to know things you don't only leads to trouble. Clients can sense when you're not being authentic, and it erodes trust quickly. I always encourage my clients to be true to themselves in their real estate decisions and financial planning. Don't buy a house just to impress others if it doesn't truly fit your needs or budget. Don't pursue investment strategies that make you uncomfortable just because they're trendy. I've seen clients find much more satisfaction and success when they make choices that align with their true selves. Remember, your home and your finances should reflect who you are, not who you think you should be.

20. The Importance of Giving Back

One of the most rewarding lessons I've learned is the value of giving back to your community. Whether it's volunteering your time, sharing your knowledge, or contributing financially, giving back enriches your life and your business in ways you can't imagine. I've seen clients find incredible opportunities and build meaningful relationships through their community involvement. In real estate, this might mean joining local housing initiatives or mentoring first-time homebuyers. Finance could involve offering free tax advice to low-income families. When you give, you often receive much more in return. It builds your reputation, expands your network, and gives you a broader perspective on your community's needs. Remember, success isn't just about what you achieve for yourself but also about the positive impact you have on others.

21. The Power of Taking Responsibility

The final lesson I want to share is perhaps the most important: take full responsibility for your actions and decisions. In real estate and tax planning, it's easy to blame others when things don't go as planned. But I've found that the most successful clients are those who own their choices, learn from their mistakes, and take charge of their futures. If a property investment doesn't work out, analyze what you could have done differently. If your tax strategy didn't yield the results you hoped for, use that as a learning experience for next year. Taking responsibility empowers you to make changes and improvements. It puts you in the driver's seat of your financial journey. Remember, you are the author of your own story. Take responsibility, learn continuously, and you'll find that success follows naturally.

As we come to the end of this journey together, I want to take a moment to thank you for allowing me to share my experiences and lessons with you. It's been a privilege to open up about my life and career, and I hope that in some way, these stories and insights have resonated with you.

You know, throughout my 46 years in real estate and tax preparation, I've come to realize that the most rewarding aspect of my work isn't just the transactions or the tax returns – it's the relationships I've built and the lives I've been able to impact positively. And that's where you come in.

If you've found value in the lessons and experiences I've shared, I'd like to ask you to consider something important. Think about the people in your life – your family, friends, and colleagues – who might be facing challenges or opportunities in real estate or tax planning. These could be individuals looking to buy their first home, sell a property, or navigate complex tax situations. By introducing them to me, you're not just helping me grow my business; you're potentially changing their lives for the better.

When you recommend me to someone you care about, you're giving them access to:

1. A trusted advisor with decades of experience in both real estate and tax preparation, offering a unique, comprehensive approach to financial decision-making.

2. Someone who prioritizes education and empowerment, ensuring your loved ones are equipped to make informed choices about their homes and finances.

3. A professional who values integrity above all else, guaranteeing honest, ethical service in every interaction.

4. A problem-solver who can navigate complex situations, potentially saving your friends and family significant time, money, and stress.

5. A compassionate guide who understands that behind every transaction and tax return is a person with hopes, dreams, and concerns.

Your referrals and recommendations are the highest compliment you can give me, and they're the lifeblood of my business. More importantly, they're an opportunity for you to make a real difference in the lives of people you care about.

As we close this book, I want to express my heartfelt gratitude to you, dear reader. Thank you for your time, your trust, and your willingness to join me on this journey of reflection and learning. Remember, your financial future and your dream home are within reach – and I'm here to help you and your loved ones every step of the way.

With warmest regards and deepest appreciation,

Laura Walker

Made in the USA
Columbia, SC
14 December 2024